T0146901

KENNEDY
OR NIXON?

THE MACMILLAN COMPANY
NEW YORK · CHICAGO
DALLAS · ATLANTA · SAN FRANCISCO
LONDON · MANILA
IN CANADA
BRETT-MACMILLAN LTD.
GALT, ONTARIO

KENNEDY OR NIXON:

*Does
it make
any
difference?*

by

ARTHUR
SCHLESINGER, JR.

New York   The Macmillan Company   1960

First Printing

The Macmillan Company, New York
Brett-Macmillan Ltd., Galt, Ontario

Printed in the United States of America

Library of Congress catalog card number: 60–16973

ISBN 978-1-5011-9938-7

If you analyze it correctly, you will conclude that our critical situation is chiefly due to men who try to please the citizens rather than to tell them what they need to hear.

—Demosthenes, trying to organize resistance among the Athenians against Philip of Macedon

FOREWORD

EVERY PRESIDENTIAL campaign has its facile and fashionable clichés. The favorite cliché of 1960 is that the two candidates, John F. Kennedy and Richard M. Nixon, are essentially the same sort of men, stamped from the same mold, committed to the same values, dedicated to the same objectives—that they are, so to speak, the Gold Dust Twins of American politics. This cliché is reinforced by the contention that, after all, there is very little to choose between their parties either—that the Democrats and Republicans have come to settle on much the same ground in domestic as well as foreign policy, that the bad old disagreements have pretty much passed away, and that, when the inquiring foreigner asks, "What is the difference between your two parties?" the honest American is impelled to answer, "Damn little any more."

This essay is an attempt to explore these clichés. It will seek to establish that there is a considerable difference between the two candidates—their personalities, their policies, their parties—and that this difference may be vital to the safety and survival of our nation in the troubled years ahead. The writer is a Democrat and a friend and partisan of Senator Kennedy; I do not pretend impartiality in this matter. But I will rest my argument whenever possible on hard and verifiable facts; and my way, I hope, will be the way of reasoned analysis, and not of appeal to prejudice or emotion.

Foreword   vii

  I   Their Personalities   1
        Nixon   2
        Kennedy   18

 II   Their Policies   35

III   Their Parties   43

KENNEDY
OR NIXON?

I   THEIR PERSONALITIES

THE CASE THAT there are no real differences in the election begins with the personalities of the candidates themselves. They are both "cool cats," we are told, men devoid of deep passions or strong convictions, sharp, ambitious, opportunistic, with no commitments except to personal advancement. They are junior executives on the make, political status seekers, end products of the Age of Public Relations. Their genius is not that of the heroic leader but of the astute manager on his way up. They represent the apotheosis of the Organization Man. "The 'managerial revolution' has come to politics," writes Eric Sevareid, "and Nixon and Kennedy are its first completely packaged products. The Processed Politician has finally arrived."

Sevareid, a member of the Kennedy-Nixon generation, recalls the exciting figures of his own youth, who "sickened at the Republic Steel massacre of strikers . . . got drunk and wept when the Spanish Republic went down . . . dreamt beautiful and foolish dreams about the perfectibility of man, cheered Roosevelt and adored the poor."

I can't find in the record that Kennedy or Nixon ever did, thought or felt these things. They must have been across the campus on Fraternity Row, with the law and business school boys, wearing the proper clothes, thinking the proper thoughts, cultivating the proper people.

I always sensed that they would end up running the big companies in town but I'm damned if I ever thought one of them would end up running the country.

As the theologian Robert E. Fitch sums it up, it is not principle but power that stands out in the character of each man, "a cool power, organized with all the skill of the calculating intellect, and disciplined by every latest device in public relations and in the manipulation of the emotions of men."

1

There can be no question too that the superficial resemblance between the two men gives this indictment an initial plausibility. Most conspicuously, Kennedy and Nixon represent the bid of the postwar generation to take over the American government. Both came of age in the 1930's. Both fought in the Second World War. Both entered politics during the Presidency of Harry S. Truman. Both showed themselves smooth, ambitious, and tough. Both dared aspire to an office held by a man who was nearly a quarter of a century old before the older of the two was born. Both callously shoved aside an entire intervening generation—the men born between 1890 and 1913—in their determined pursuit of the presidential prize. The sight of these brash young men knocking with such confidence on the door of the White House comes as a natural shock to a nation—indeed, to a world—used to government by the elders.

In addition, both men, as Eric Sevareid has pointed out, were exempt from the emotions which swept so many young men of the thirties (though one wonders how relevant this point really is: it is not on the record that Woodrow Wilson or Franklin Roosevelt spent much time marching on picket lines in their youth). Both, too, take a cool, professional pleasure in politics for its own sake—an interesting development after a decade in which the moral premium has been placed on being "above" politics. Yet, when one has said these things, and adds that both are males, husbands, fathers, and that both have given the impression of a certain reserve in personal contacts, one has, in my judgment, about exhausted the catalogue of resemblances. Beyond this, Kennedy and Nixon seem to me vastly different in their interests, their skills, and their motivations.

NIXON

LET US FIRST consider Richard Nixon. He is in one respect unique among major American politicians of this century. Every other major political leader within memory is identified with substantive positions of one sort or another on issues; every other about what is intellectually or morally the right or wrong position to take on questions of public policy. Stewart Alsop, a friendly biographer, sums up Nixon's role in the Eisenhower administration as recorded in Robert Donovan's revealing book *Eisenhower: The Inside Story:* "When an issue is up for discussion, Nixon shrewdly sums up the probable political impact of alternative courses of action—he very rarely comments on the inherent merits of the issue in question." Only such a man could become the presidential candidate of a party the day after he received his political program at the hands of his chief rival for the nomination.

4

BECAUSE HE HAS no political philosophy, he has no sense of history. One feels about Nixon that he is disembodied, not only in relation to any inward substance of conviction, but also in relation to the past experience of his own country. When Khrushchev, in the famous dialogue in the kitchen, asked whether America has not existed for three hundred years and Nixon replied, no, one hundred and fifty, thereby founding his country in 1809, one felt that both were entirely creatures of their particular time, with no roots in the past and with only the haziest notions of history.

No one with a sense of tradition could have done what Nixon did in the years 1950–1954, thinking it good clean fun to identify his political opponents with treason to the Republic. Not that American politics has not traditionally been lively and uninhibited. Our politicians have always enjoyed a considerable latitude in polemic and invective. But one line of attack has always been considered unforgivable—that is, to question the patriotism of those with whom one disagreed about public policy. "One can criticize, slash hard, accuse opponents of stupidity, blindness, inefficiency— any number of things," as *Commonweal* once put it in an editorial. "But it is impossible to imply that one's opponents deliberately betrayed the interests of the United States, and then expect to be able to work with these men after the campaign is over as if nothing had happened." Today Nixon, looking back on the days when he used to characterize Truman, Stevenson, and Acheson as the supporters and defenders of the Communist conspiracy, is said to express (in private) a certain rueful regret; but he has never indicated any real understanding of the enormity of his offense. He seems now to dismiss it all as a youthful excess, not appropriate perhaps to the dignity of a Vice President, but still essentially (in one of his cherished phrases) just "a fighting, rocking, socking campaign" in the American way. He seems not to understand that false imputations of disloyalty have never been in the American way. He seems not to understand that he is the only major American politician in our history who came to prominence by techniques which, if generally adopted, would destroy the whole fabric of mutual confidence on which democracy rests. If he understood such things, he would understand better why traditional American politicians like Sam Rayburn, instead of accepting his protestations that he was just a good, free-swinging, hard-hitting American boy, continue to regard him with incredulity and contempt.

The "other-directed" man lacks a sense of history. In its place, because his own relationship with the world is at once passive and manipulative, he tends to put an instinctive belief in fatalism and in conspiracy. Nixon typically combines a naïve determinism ("I'm fatalistic about politics. . . . What happens is in the lap of the Fates") with a marked susceptibility to the conspiratorial interpretation. Anyone who has studied history knows that most historical phenomena are the consequence of tendency and accident—that very few events can be traced to the secret machinations of a small coterie of evil individuals. Yet, if Nixon's mind contains no steady deposit of conviction, one feels that it contains a rather steady commitment to form; and that nothing is more pervasive in the way he thinks than his addiction to the conspiratorial view of things.

This was bold and explicit in the 1950–1954 period, when he saw recent world history as a product of a conspiracy of Communists and recent American history as a product of a conspiracy of members of Americans for Democratic Action. His automatic reaction when first challenged about his fund in 1952 is revealing: "I was warned that if I continued to attack the Communists and crooks in this government they would continue to smear me, and, believe me, you can expect that they will continue to do so. They started it yesterday." Since 1954, he has generally repressed public avowal of conspiratorial obsessions. He seems to understand that too much talk in such terms is considered bad taste. But one has the uneasy feeling that the conspiratorial interpretation still lurks underneath the surface of his reactions. He is always on the verge of pronouncing himself the victim of some clandestine plot. Occasionally this impulse breaks through. Thus in September, 1958, *The New York Times* addressed a routine inquiry to the State Department as to how the mail was running on government policy during the Quemoy-Matsu crisis. The Department replied that 80 per cent of the letters received were critical of administration policy. At this point, the Vice President suddenly intervened. He issued a formal statement, declaring himself "shocked" to read that "the preponderance of mail to the State Department opposed the policy the United States is following with Quemoy and Matsu." He then denounced "the patent and deliberate effort of a State Department subordinate to undercut the Secretary of State and sabotage his policy"—that is, by telling the truth to *The New York Times?* Here, one feels, is the spontaneous Nixon mode of interpreting unpleasant events. Somewhere, he seems instinctively to feel, there is some person or clique deliberately doing wicked things; if one could only identify the villain and lower the boom on him, then everything would be all right.

5

HIS BIOGRAPHERS HAVE made much of the fact that Nixon is a lonely man, that he has few intimates, that he finds it hard to establish hail-fellow-well-met relations with the gang. Some suggest that this is the majestic loneliness of a Washington or Lincoln. But the "other-directed" man is, of course, a lonely man: hence the title of the Riesman book.

In adult life he continues to respond to [his] peers, not only with overt conformity, as do people in all times and places, but also in a deeper sense, in the very quality of his feeling. Yet, paradoxically, he remains a lonely member of the crowd because he never comes really close to the others or to himself.

"Other-directed" people strive constantly to escape this pervading loneliness. A favorite resort in such circumstances is to what Riesman calls "false personalization"—that is, the compulsion to "personalize" relations which are inherently and properly impersonal, to give a spurious personal content to relationships which exist on quite other bases. Politics has always had a personal element; any great leader exerts an attraction which spills over the policy questions technically at issue. But the "false personalization" which has recently overtaken our politics has gone beyond simply the personal magnetism of the leader.

An example, trivial but symptomatic, will make the point. One may go through all the collected papers of all the Presidents of the United States, and one will never find in any formal address a reference by any President to his wife—not, that is to say, till the 1950's. George Washington never said how glad "Martha and I" were for the tributes of the crowd, nor did Lincoln announce his gratitude to Mary Todd, nor did Franklin Roosevelt—and he might well have paid a tribute to a wife who, more than most First Ladies, was a collaborator in policy matters—allude on formal occasions to his Eleanor. The Republican convention of 1960 provided a revealing contrast. President Eisenhower spoke so glowingly of Mamie that one got the impression that she was a leading figure in the Republican Party herself. No doubt this was a generous and gallant touch by the President, but was it really appropriate? Should a President not be content to rest his case on his public record? or must we expect Presidents ever after to cast their family lives also into the scales, as if this constituted a further achievement of their administration? People have said that President Eisenhower has not been an innovator; but here at least he has departed from precedent.

The Vice President seems determined to follow in his footsteps. I bet a Republican friend that, when Nixon gave his acceptance address, he would mention his wife before his fourth sentence. Pat appeared in the second sentence. Indeed, Nixon speeches regularly begin with a "Pat-and-I" phrase. One can understand all this as the effort of the lonely man to try to humanize his relationship with the crowd. Still, charging politics with such pseudopersonal matter is irrelevant: it puts the political process on a wholly false basis. More than that, it is degrading: by catering to and thus cultivating irrelevant emotions, it corrupts the political dialogue. It construes politics, not as the means by which a free people conduct their affairs, but as a form of soap opera. It presumes the people incapable of understanding the real facts of anything: everything has to be made simple, dramatic, emotional, explained in familiar and childish terms or explained away entirely.

The hard fact is that Nixon lacks taste. This may sound like a frivolous comment. It is not. Taste goes to the heart of the relationship between the politician and the people: a leader's taste can uplift or debase the level of his country's politics. Nor by taste do I mean the urbanity acquired on the Eastern seaboard or at an Ivy League college. I mean an instinct for dignity—for one's own dignity, and for the dignity of others. Andrew Jackson did not go to Harvard, but he had such an instinct. No one with such an instinct could say things that Nixon has said: no one with respect for others could suppose that others would be moved by them.* One thinks, of course, of the Checkers speech of 1952; but I would be prepared to relinquish this speech to the statute of limitations. There is an abundance of more recent examples, a number from convention week, 1960. Who can forget Nixon's account of how he prepared for his acceptance address? I spent a week, he said, reading philosophy and political science and his-

* There are those who will say that Harry S. Truman was also a man without taste. It may be that, in his capacity as a private citizen, when outraged, for example, by the heresies of a music critic, Mr. Truman behaved without taste. It is true also that on the hustings Mr. Truman could give 'em hell in the best Populist tradition (though he never, of course, questioned the loyalty or patriotism of his political opponents). And I did not like his Key West shirts either. But, as a public servant, Mr. Truman always showed vast respect for the dignity of his office. He did not exploit his wife, his daughter, or his dog in order to make political points or to advance his political fortunes. Moreover, as a public servant, Mr. Truman always showed respect for the intelligence of the people and their capacity to understand great issues and rise to great challenges.

tory; then I sat down and wrote the speech. The whole utterance is authentic Nixon. In the first place, it is evident that he did not do what he said he did; no one who had read such works would talk about them this way (he would say, "I read Kant and Burke and Macaulay"). In the second place, the speech itself, far from showing any evidence of prolonged immersion in the classics, was simply an amalgamation of speeches the Vice President had been pretesting up and down the country for the last six months.

It is hard to define the precise Nixonian quality. One word for it is "corny," but the matter is far more complicated than that. Thus, when assailed by an angry mob in Peru, Nixon spoke of the occasion as "a day that will live in infamy." This, as Evelyn Houston pointed out in a perceptive comment, was characteristic of the Vice President's taste—first, "in plagiarizing the terrible dignity" of a phrase reserved for all time for Pearl Harbor Sunday, and then in equating the threats of Peruvian hoodlums against his own person with acts of aggression by one nation against another. Moreover, when Nixon was warned of trouble at the University, he decided to go anyway, saying "They can't frighten me." This, Miss Houston suggests, was language for a certain scale—for a private quarrel, a personal threat. But was it appropriate for the second official of a great nation? Do we expect him to show cowardice so that he must promise us he won't? "Could it ever have occurred to Winston Churchill in the dark hours of 1940 to assure his people that he was a brave man? He took for granted that men are brave."

"It is the style of Nixon," Miss Houston concludes, "or to be more painfully exact, the lack of one—that pervasive and alchemic falsity, which isn't art or showmanship, a respectable talent, but a veritable Midas touch for making ersatz of the real, that has made many of us wince. . . . It isn't the in-fighting, it isn't the instinct for the jugular, it isn't even the smiling face that luck seems always to have turned upon him. These things are real and can be resisted as real. It is the mechanizing, the demeaning, the patronizing of our perceptions and sensibilities, the subtle corruption, which I used to think was calculated by him but have come to believe is in great part unconscious, of communication on the level where we perceive not Americans, not highbrow or lowbrow, conformist or heretic, but each other. His brains and vigor might pull us out of this mess, but how could men come large again for a leader whose own eyes so plainly reflect them diminished?"

6

THE KEY TO Nixon is provided by the word to which he has been so long devoted—the word "image." A serious man does not spend time fussing about the image he presents to the public. He knows that, for better or for worse, he is what he is. His identity is secure. He can't transform himself, and he can't hope to persuade others that he is different from what he is. The "other-directed" man, however, has no sure sense of his own identity: he is real, even for himself, only as he sees himself reflected in the eyes of others; he thus perceives himself, not as an individual, but as an image.

No political leader in the history of the Republic has exhibited so consistent and extraordinary a self-consciousness about the figure he cuts in public as Nixon. In his confidences to friendly biographers, like Earl Mazo, he candidly portrays himself as a man whose every move is considered and calculated.

The minute I stepped off the airplane . . . I cased the place. I always do that when I walk out. I looked it all over and watched the kind of crowd, thinking where will I make an unscheduled stop, where will we move out and shake hands, and so forth.

When dealing with this type of situation, your mind must always go, even while you're shaking hands and going through all the maneuvers. I developed the ability long ago to do one thing while thinking of another.

You have to be very careful in a situation like that. You have to think all those things through.

The most difficult period in one of these incidents is not in handling the situation at the time. The difficult task is with your reactions after it is all over. I get a real letdown after one of these issues. Then I begin

to think of what real bums they are. You also get the sense that you
licked them. . . . Then you try to catch yourself . . . to be a generous winner. Most importantly you must think of what the lasting
impression is going to be.

And no one can ever forget his remark to Ralph de Toledano:
"The only time to lose your temper in politics is when it's deliberate." The objection is not so much to the behavior: some such
thoughts probably run at one time or other through the minds of
most public figures. The objection is to the fantastic energy and
solemnity Nixon dedicates to such analysis of his behavior. His
stream of consciousness is obviously dominated, not by any concern for issues—no public question receives anywhere near so
minute and comprehensive an analysis as do his own acts—but by
the manipulation of his own public "image"; not by content, but
by appearances; least of all by a sense of humor.

Little in our recent political literature is more symptomatic, and
more genuinely pathetic, than the spate of stories which the Vice
President gave the press in July during the Republican convention
and on his subsequent trip to Hawaii. A headline in the *New York
Herald Tribune* put it concisely: "Nixon's Aim: To Portray Himself as a Regular Guy." The Vice President's object, Warren
Rogers, Jr., wrote in one story, could be authoritatively stated as
follows: "1. To build a public image of a fighting underdog, a man
of the people, to whom all things come hard. 2. By contrast, to
picture . . . Kennedy . . . as a rich man's son, born with a silver
spoon in his mouth." Rogers then offered examples of the way
Nixon has set about to establish these theses.

One night after a steak dinner, the Vice President told reporters and
live television cameras, "I really prefer hamburgers. I really do."
   Another time at a victory celebration with the California delegation,
he said, "I don't like champagne, even California champagne."

The use of the word "even" in the last line is a deft Nixon touch.
   The developing Nixon image, wrote Gladwin Hill in the *Times,*
was especially to be tinctured with the "humble bit"—frequent
references to his own and his wife's lean childhood days. "For

example, 'grinding hamburgers in my father's little grocery store in Yerba Linda—and it was good hamburger, too.' " "If anybody had any doubts about the American dream," Nixon told Earl Mazo of the *Herald Tribune* in a manner which even that friendly reporter could not but describe as solemn, "they ought to look at us." "Us," of course, were Pat-and-I. With an air of magnanimity, the Vice President stuck his opponent with qualities he wistfully denied himself, such as being a "natural smiler" and as glamour boy. But, as Rogers wrote in the *Herald Tribune,* Nixon feels that "he can turn the Kennedy assets into liabilities, contrasting his own humble, plodding, serious, lonely—*he would like it to be called Lincolnesque*—manner with that of the wealthy, flashy, handsome, sometimes imperious Kennedy clan" (*New York Herald Tribune,* August 7, 1960, my italics).

What has all this to do with making sure that government of the people, by the people, for the people shall not perish from the earth? Can one think of any President who began his campaign for high office by conducting fascinated discussions of his own "image" and entreating that his personality be thereafter described as Lincolnesque? This is surely the act of a man in desperate quest of identity—a quest so absorbing that it shoulders aside all public issues. Nothing else seems much to preoccupy him, neither America's decline in the world, nor the problems generated by our population boom at home, nor the plight of the Negroes or of the farmers; only Pat-and-I as a certification of the American dream, and how the Nixon image compares to the Kennedy image.

7

RICHARD NIXON IS not a bad man. He will not grind down the faces of the poor. He will not institute a police state. His mind is stocked with a collection of conservative aphorisms and attitudes; other things being equal, he follows them, but he doesn't believe in them too strongly. He would make a better President than men like Goldwater or Knowland, although they have a larger degree of inner conviction. Yet he remains a strangely hollow man. He lacks a solid sense of his own identity—"no foundation, all the way down the line," as the character said in the Saroyan play. He lacks too a solid sense of history. In addition, he is wanting in fineness of personal grain; either he is a cynical faker (which he surely is not), or his emotional range and language are genuinely that of the world of soap opera. His only passion is the passion to win.

Nixon is in many respects a good example of midcentury man, obsessed with appearances rather than with the reality of things, obsessed above all with his own appearance, his own image, seeking reassurance through winning, but never knowing why he is so mad to win or what he will do with his victory. Issues for him are subordinate and secondary, to be maneuvered and manipulated. What matters is stance, not substance: what matters is a felt righteousness of motive, a sentence of humility on the lips, a look of dedication on the face.

One may well ask: what happens to such a man in the moment of stark crisis when public issues become irreducible and nothing can meet them except a rock-bottom philosophy of politics and life?

KENNEDY

IF THIS IS the way Nixon is, then it is clear that Kennedy could hardly be more different. For the essential fact about Kennedy is that 'he cares about the reality of issues—that he is an intelligent man and that his intelligence is devoted to trying to find out what the best answer to any given problem is. The electorate, moreover, sees him as identified with specific positions and specific policies. Nixon can change his mind about almost anything without violating the public conception of himself. Can Kennedy? Kennedy has changed his mind conspicuously in one area—agricultural policy. For a time he was a supporter of Ezra Benson. Eventually he altered his position, either because J. K. Galbraith and other economists convinced him that Benson was wrong on the merits, or because it was politically disastrous to be for Benson: both reasons no doubt played their part. On everything else, Kennedy, unlike Nixon, has had a consistent record over the last seven years. Apply the change-of-mind test to Kennedy. If he were, for example, suddenly to come out in favor of the French in Algeria, or to praise Jimmy Hoffa as a labor statesman, or to demand the inclusion of a loyalty oath in education bills, or to denounce medical aid to the aged as socialized medicine, this would cause a public shock. Nixon can change about freely and safely; Kennedy can't. Nixon, in short, is perceived and accepted as a chameleon; Kennedy, as a man of some steadfastness of conviction. If both men appear at times cool in their attitude toward issues, this is, I would say, because Kennedy reasons about them and Nixon doesn't much care.

One ground on which Kennedy admires Stevenson is Stevenson's conviction that issues are too important to be fooled around with for political purposes. Kennedy was present at a meeting in a Boston hotel shortly after Suez in 1956 when a group of potential contributors to the Democratic Party tried to persuade Stevenson to take a position on the Middle Eastern crisis which Stevenson thought was wrong. A lesser politician, Kennedy feels, would have gone along with what was wanted, especially in the confused closing days of a campaign. Stevenson refused to do so and explained cogently why such behavior seemed to him reckless and unworthy. This incident has remained in Kennedy's mind as an example of the proper relationship between issues and politics. In short, for Nixon issues are secondary to politics, for Kennedy politics tend to be secondary to issues.

2

BECAUSE HE CARES about issues, Kennedy has a sense of history—or, more likely, the relationship is in reverse: because he has a sense of history, he cares about issues. He has neither Nixon's fatalism nor his penchant for conspiratorial explanations. He understands that history is an intricate combination of fatality and fortuity on which the will of the leader can at times operate with decisive effect. He believes that, within limits, the intelligence of man can affect the course of events.

Hence his interest in issues is not only curative but preventive. He has regularly devoted speeches, for example, to topics whose only significance lies in the remote future. He manifestly takes the time to study and, more important, to think, about issues far in advance of packaged and hackneyed opinion, because they interest *him* and strike *him* as crucial—whether or not anyone in the audience is ready to respond or to appreciate. Indeed, he seems to understand that preparing the people for what is going to overtake them in the future, and for the demands they are going to have to fill, is one of the highest duties of the political leader.

Thus he was an early voice calling attention to the gathering crisis in Indo-China and urging independence for Vietnam, Laos, and Cambodia—a policy which France eventually followed, almost too late to do any good. An even more celebrated instance was his speech in 1957 on Algeria. This was far from a vote-catching speech: the number of Algerian voters in the United States is limited. More than that, the speech did Kennedy genuine political harm. It brought down upon him the wrath of the Establishment in foreign policy, led by former Secretary of State Dean Acheson. The Council on Foreign Relations mentality was outraged by what was termed an irresponsible attack on the policies of our French ally; after all, Henry Cabot Lodge and Douglas Dillon had expressed firm faith in the French Government's handling of the matter, and that should have been that.

Rereading the Kennedy speech today, one wonders what all the shouting was about. It is a moderate and prophetic forecast of the evolution of events in North Africa. It ably sets forth the position toward which De Gaulle has been moving since his return to power; if French governments had adopted it when Kennedy first advocated it, the Algerian crisis would have been much closer to solution. As for the alleged "irresponsibility" of the speech, the only test of that is whether it strengthened or weakened those inside France working for a more rational approach. I happened to be in Paris when the speech was delivered and can testify that it was received with gratitude by the opponents of the now discredited

Algerian policy. Jean-Jacques Servan-Schreiber ran the entire text in *L'Express*. When Kennedy said, "Algeria is no longer a problem for the French alone—nor will it ever be again," he signaled the increasing concern of the Atlantic community in the Algerian affair. The French critics of the policy felt that only evidence of such concern could force a revision of the policy. Unfortunately, too few voices echoed Kennedy outside France, and no revision took place until De Gaulle came to power. In any case, can one cite any speech of Nixon's that provoked a comparable discussion of serious issues? *

One can multiply the examples. Kennedy's speech of 1958 on Latin America contained a detailed indictment of the policies which have come to such melancholy fruition in the tragedy of Cuba. "An announced policy of nonintervention," Kennedy said, "becomes a sham when it is turned off and on to suit our own purposes. It should apply to businessmen as well as to diplomats, to economic as well as political revolution." The nonintervention policy, he said, must not "tie our hands completely with respect to dictatorships in Latin America." He called on the State Department to give Latin American affairs higher priority. And he urged a larger measure of United States economic aid—but aid to be employed by Latin Americans, he emphasized, "within their own political and economic framework. They resent our insisting upon a larger role for their private enterprise, which cannot cope with many of their problems, or a larger role for our private investors." One paragraph deserves thoughtful reading today:

Investment in a growing area, rich in resource potential—an area which asks not for a charity handout but for financial arrangements in which its members are willing to participate—is not throwing money down the drain. On the contrary, our dollars spent in Latin America return to pay for our goods and services. Ninety-eight cents of every American dollar spent to purchase sugar from Cuba, for example, is spent by the Cubans to buy American exports. And we can be certain that any vacuum we leave through the instability of our own foreign trade policies will be swiftly filled by the Soviet Union.

* The full text of the speech is to be found in John F. Kennedy, *The Strategy of Peace* (New York, 1960), pp. 65–81.

The problem of "underdevelopment" constitutes the crux of world politics in the sixties. Kennedy knows this and has worked hard to understand the limits and the possibilities of American action in the underdeveloped world. Thus no Senator has done more to promote American aid to India. Indeed, where in the entire Nixon lexicon can one match this prescient statesmanship of Kennedy on Indo-China and India, on Algeria and Latin America? Kennedy has similarly advocated a more intelligent economic policy toward nations behind the Iron Curtain. And Kennedy has shown equal readiness to advance politically unfamiliar issues in the domestic field. His speech to the National Press Club last winter on the Presidency was an effort to transfer a subject of highest importance from the American Political Science Association to the forum of popular debate.

All these issues, whether in domestic policy or foreign, were issues which Kennedy selected, not because political market research told him that the electorate cared about them, but because he, John F. Kennedy, thought they damn well ought to care. This is surely an essential responsibility of leadership in a democracy.

3

KENNEDY THUS STANDS in sharp contrast to Nixon in possessing a genuine, rather than a manipulative, interest in issues and ideas. By whatever test one applies, Kennedy has shown a penetrating and persistent concern with the substance of problems; while Nixon, in Stewart Alsop's phrase, "very rarely comments on the inherent merits of the issue in question." This is further exhibited by their contrasting relationships with the intellectual community.

Kennedy himself is a bookish man. He not only writes books, but he reads them, inveterately and eclectically. He is interested in intellectual discussion. He is not precisely an intellectual himself, but, like Franklin D. Roosevelt, he can enjoy the company of intellectuals with perfect confidence in his capacity to hold his own. From an early point in his political career he turned to the academic resources of the nation in order to check and clarify his thinking on public policy.

Nixon's history in this respect is altogether different. He is not on record as a great reader. His friendly biographers Mr. Mazo and Mr. Alsop do not even bother to claim that he has read much in history or economics or political philosophy (and, when he makes that claim for himself, it is self-evidently spurious). During his political life in the House and Senate, he never made use of the resources of the great California universities, as Kennedy turned instinctively to Harvard and the Massachusetts Institute of Technology. As Vice President, he showed no interest in the intellectuals of the country. In such a matter as the repeal of the disclaimer affidavit in the Defense Education Act, it required the most intense pressure from Republican university presidents to elicit from Nixon a perfunctory statement in support of the Kennedy-Clark bill.

Once Nixon became a presidential candidate, of course, everything appeared to change. With considerable éclat, a brain trust was formed and an egghead committee was launched. I would say nothing invidious about Scholars for Nixon, whose leaders include my distinguished colleagues William Yandell Elliott and Lon Fuller, except to assert that pro-Nixonism is a minority position in the American scholarly community. As for Nixon's own last-minute enthusiasm for intellectual support, one can only attribute this to a great change in the national mood to which, with "other-directed" precision, he now seeks to conform. In 1952 the egghead was a figure of scorn. Now, it would seem, a presidential candidate feels naked if he ventures into a campaign without an accompanying troupe of intellectuals.

I cannot believe that anyone will be deceived by this Nixon conversion. Kennedy's desire to work with the intellectual community long predated his interest in the Presidency. If he should be defeated for the Presidency, his collaboration will continue. It is an organic part of his approach to politics. Nixon's bones cast to the intellectuals are a transparent piece of campaign opportunism.

4

IT SHOULD BE evident that Kennedy is an exceptionally cerebral figure. By this I mean that his attitudes proceed to an unusual degree from dispassionate rational analysis. If elected, he will be the most purely cerebral President we have had since Woodrow Wilson. "Purely cerebral" is in this case a relative term. Wilson's rationalism masked deep passions, and Kennedy has the normal human quota of sympathy and prejudice. There are weaknesses too in such a broad reliance on cerebration. Still, compared to most politicians, Kennedy has habits of thought which are unusually detached, consecutive, and explicit. His mind is a first-class instrument, strong, supple, disciplined.

For a long time, however, Kennedy's intelligence was underemployed. He grew up; he went to Choate; he went to Harvard. At Harvard he seemed a light and agreeable figure; then, toward the end of his college career, he began to come to life intellectually. He took his degree with honors and converted his honors essay into the book, *Why England Slept,* published in 1940. Then came the war; after the war came politics. As a Kennedy, he had to do better than anyone else. But it all seemed rather a game, in which one tried hard to win but avoided taking it all too seriously. Why this slight tinge of unreality in his early political career? Perhaps it was connected with the illnesses that had assailed him since the war; perhaps he felt that his life might be short and he had better enjoy it while he could.

He was still rather an unformed man even when he was elected to the Senate in 1952 at the age of thirty-five. He was bright and quick, but he had not resolved the problem of his own style, his own identity. Then came the series of operations on his back in 1955—a double fusion of spinal discs with ensuing complications. He nearly died; last rites were pronounced; but he survived and in the end the most troubling of his ailments were definitely cured. From the moment he knew he was sure to live, ambition, I imagine, took over from enjoyment, and he decided that he could be President of the United States. Like Roosevelt's polio, Kennedy's nearly fatal sickness of 1955 no doubt accelerated his private crisis of identity. Like Roosevelt, he emerged more focused, more purposeful, more formidable. He began to convey an impression of personal weight and authority.

His intelligence now had a goal. For the first time it swung into full action. The character of Kennedy's mind is worth considering. If it is less scholarly than Wilson's, less bold and adventurous than Franklin Roosevelt's, less rich and reflective than Adlai Stevenson's, it has nonetheless qualities of its own. His intelligence is sharp, analytical, practical, and unfettered. He thinks constantly in terms of problems and is willing to consider anything that promises a secure solution. This determined his approach to the Presidency. He began to look at the position of the United States; and the thing that came to strike him most forcibly was the discrepancy between our national potential and our national performance—between the amplitude of wealth and talent and resources, on the one hand, and our lagging positions in economic growth, defense, education, social welfare, on the other. How was this discrepancy to be overcome? Everything, as Kennedy looked at it, went back to the question of Presidential leadership. What was necessary, it seemed to him, was some means of steering more of our national abundance into the things that build the economic and military and moral power of the nation—and that means could only be affirmative government directed by a strong President. The convergence of intelligence and ambition thus gave Kennedy an increasingly coherent political philosophy.

5

PEOPLE ASK, "Is Kennedy a committed liberal?" The answer, in my judgment, is yes. But what about McCarthy? Kennedy's record on McCarthy, as I told him at the time, seemed to me discreditable. Nor can I accept the argument that a more aggressive anti-McCarthy position would have involved him in serious political trouble in Massachusetts. Brien McMahon with a similar constituency was moving before his death toward an anti-McCarthy position in Connecticut. It can be argued, I think, that John Kennedy was in a uniquely strong position to oppose McCarthy. When one condemns his silence, however, several other points should be made. For one thing, very few Senators, including very few of the liberal Senators, spoke up against McCarthy in 1950–1953. For another, though Kennedy was silent, he was not sympathetic; he was never, like Nixon, a collaborator with McCarthy. He never has been obsessed with Communism as an internal threat, and he has never had Nixon's susceptibility to the conspiratorial interpretation of history. On the secondary issues connected with McCarthyism, Kennedy voted with regularity against the Wisconsin Senator; he voted for the confirmation of Charles E. Bohlen and James B. Conant; he voted against the confirmation of Scott McLeod and Robert E. Lee. He was prepared in August, 1954, to vote for censure; when the vote was delayed to December Kennedy lay gravely ill in the hospital. Kennedy's misfortune was that, by writing a book entitled *Profiles in Courage,* he invited particular attention to his own circumspection in the McCarthy period.

Since 1950–1953, Kennedy has clarified his conception of the place of individual freedom and due process in a democracy. He has shown this in his defense of the Supreme Court and in his fight against the loyalty affidavit in the Defense Education Act. Today he seems to me a committed liberal. But he is not particularly committed by spontaneous visceral reactions in the usual pattern of American liberals. He is committed rather by intellectual analysis —by his conviction that history requires certain things of the United States, and that these things can be achieved only by programs of the kind which are conventionally known as liberal. He thus comes to liberalism by a different road from that of most liberals. But his conclusions are no less solidly grounded or less firmly held.

As I suggested earlier, there are disadvantages in being so predominantly cerebral. Men like Roosevelt, in whom ratiocination was informed by intuition and enriched by feeling, can often both understand more and communicate more than the coldly analytical types. But intellectual commitment can provide the framework for feeling. "Some people have their liberalism 'made' by the time they reach their late twenties," Kennedy once said. "I didn't. I was caught in cross currents and eddies. It was only later that I got into the stream of things." Once Kennedy resolved the problem of his own identity, his own emotions were liberated for an increasingly forceful commitment to liberalism.

Campaigning in West Virginia, for example, gave his social views a new concreteness. He had read a good deal about poverty, but like most other Americans he had never seen fellow country-men living the way unemployed miners and their families are living today in West Virginia; and the sight struck home with peculiar force because it fitted squarely into his general feeling that America was not realizing its own potential. Where Nixon can minimize such suffering as the price one pays for the free enterprise system, where he can deny that the national government can properly do much to contribute to the relief of distressed areas, Kennedy saw the poverty of West Virginia as an abomination to the Republic—and one which national power could remedy. He had long argued in the Senate for the Democratic bill on area redevelopment. Now it seemed more imperative than ever. West Virginia is only one ex-ample: ever since Kennedy has worked out his general philosophy, one sees in him a visible growth into commitment on many fronts.

6

THE CONTRAST between Kennedy and Nixon with regard to the substance of policy—issues and ideas—could hardly be more clear-cut. The contrast in political styles, I would suggest, is equally definite. Nixon, we have seen, is an expert practitioner of "false personalization." He imports histrionics into politics. His rhetoric is vulgar. He exhorts, denounces, parades emotional irrele-vances, even weeps. Kennedy's political manner, on the other hand, is studiously unemotional, impersonal, antihistrionic. He has no scruples about using his family as part of his political organization, but he does not lug them into his serious speeches.

Let us try a test: can anyone imagine Kennedy giving the Checkers speech? The equivalent of that speech for Kennedy was his reply to Harry Truman shortly before the 1960 convention. The two speeches are worth a moment's comparison. In each case, the speaker was attempting to counter a head-on personal indict-ment in a hectic, last-minute crisis. Nixon's approach was wholly subjective: it was to present a version of his life in terms calculated to rouse sentimental sympathy for himself and his family. It is not clear what his war record had to do with the California fund, but he could say, with fake modesty, "I was just there when the bombs were falling." (This statement forced even so friendly a commentator as Stewart Alsop to note, "Since Nixon had a non-combat job far from the battle lines, there presumably were not many bombs.") His wife, his children, his dog were all grist to his mill. And to this day Nixon remains so proud of the speech that he celebrates the day of its delivery as an anniversary.

Kennedy's approach, on the other hand, was objective. His speech consisted of a careful, low-keyed analysis of the merits of the issue of youth in history and logic. It was almost wholly devoid of autobiography, theatrics, or personal pleading. It did not exploit his authentic war heroism. It represented, not an assault on the emotions of his audience, but an appeal for rational deliberation and judgment.

This question of taste, as I have suggested earlier, is far from irrelevant. It helps determine the level of political discourse. Kennedy is noncorny. His is the world, not of the sob story, nor of the high school debater, but of serious men trying to find serious solutions to serious problems.

This is related, of course, to their respective senses of identity. One finds in Kennedy none of Nixon's almost morbid preoccupation with the techniques of personal projection. One finds none of the Nixon-like flood of self-conscious concern over the "image" he presents to the public. Can anyone imagine Nixon opening up his files for unrestricted use by a distinguished and independent-minded scholar in the preparation of a biography, as Kennedy did when he gave Professor James MacGregor Burns of Williams, the noted political scientist, free access to his papers? Kennedy has evidently come to terms with himself and believes that what he has to say is more important than how he says it. He cannot disavow his age, his money, his looks, his college, his father, his intellect, his religion, his self-possession, or even his sense that he can achieve what needs to be achieved more effectively than almost anyone else on the scene. Therefore he presents himself with exactitude as he is, giving his critics who cry "cold" and "machinelike" the target they desire, but gradually accustoming the rest of us to the particular strengths of his brand of personality.

7

ONE POINT IS often made in the Kennedy-Nixon comparison—that is, the point of "experience." "There is no man in the history of America," President Eisenhower has said of Nixon, "who has had such careful preparation . . . for carrying out the duties of the Presidency." Of course, one might well first inquire what the nature of this experience has been. If it is experience in helping bring about a decline in our relative national power, a slow-up in our economic growth and a condition of national moral lassitude, this may well be a kind of experience which we no longer need. But let us construe the question more literally. Has Nixon, in fact, been better prepared for the Presidency than any man in history?

This argument hinges in part on a myth that Nixon, as Vice President, has been given greater executive and policy responsibility than any previous Vice President. Any such assertion is demonstrably untrue. The hard fact is that Henry A. Wallace as Vice President in 1941–1945 had far more executive responsibility than Nixon has had. Wallace ran the Supply, Priorities, and Allocation Board and later the Board of Economic Welfare. Not only has Nixon had no comparable administrative jobs; he has been given no real executive assignments at all. Moreover, Wallace had behind him eight years as Secretary of Agriculture. And, if foreign travel is a component of "experience," Wallace also went on his share of foreign missions. His trip to Latin America, for example, was considerably more successful than Nixon's. If the Vice Presidential experience constitutes an argument for Nixon in 1960, it constituted a much stronger argument for Wallace in 1948. How many who affect to be impressed by it now were impressed by it then?

The "experience" argument is urged most strongly in the foreign field. Actually, if this argument were to be taken seriously, it would help Kennedy more than it would Nixon. No American newspaperman has followed the formulation of foreign policy more carefully than James Reston of *The New York Times*. Mr. Reston recently wrote, "Senator Kennedy has probably been a deeper student of foreign affairs for longer than the Vice President." From *Why England Slept* in 1940 to *The Strategy of Peace* in 1960 he has maintained a lively interest in international affairs. He has been an unusually active member of a distinguished Senate Foreign Relations Committee. He has proposed new programs of legislation in a multitude of areas—aid to the underdeveloped world, disarmament, India, Algeria, Indo-China, NATO, Western Europe, Eastern Europe, Formosa Straits, Latin America, Africa.

Against this, Nixon has little to show. His concern with foreign affairs is relatively recent. His foreign policy speeches—with the exception of foreign aid, on which he has spoken forthrightly, if with illusions about the extent to which private investment can take up the slack—are jejune and boring. Those who make a case for Nixon against Kennedy in foreign policy are forced to cite principally his "experience" in forming basic policy within the administration and his "experience" in conducting foreign missions for the President. Both forms of experience, alas, vanish when approached for closer examination.

What experience has Nixon had in forming basic policy within the administration? He attends meetings of the National Security Council, it is true; but the investigations of the Jackson Committee show that the National Security Council has become more and more a ceremonial body, and that the critical national decisions are generally taken outside it. Not only are they taken outside the NSC; they are also taken outside the Vice President. Eisenhower recently put it with candor concerning Nixon: "He was not a part of decision-making." The record abundantly justifies the Presidential disclaimer. Indeed, Nixon himself has several times exposed by public utterance his astonishing ignorance of vital foreign policy decisions already made by the Eisenhower administration. One remembers, for example, his support of military intervention in Indo-China in 1954. It became immediately evident that the administration had no such policy. The State Department disowned the Vice President the next day. In a short time, with his customary facility, he was disowning himself.

But this was 1954. Let us take a look then at the most spectacu-
lar foreign policy crisis of 1960—the U-2 affair. If the Vice President had been carefully trained all these years for his impending
responsibilities, here, one would think, on the verge of his transla-
tion to ultimate authority, he would play a leading role. Or, if he
did not play a leading role, then at least people would tell him what
was going on. But what happened? On the evening of May 15, on
the television show "Open End," Nixon not only defended the
flights but advocated their continuance. Such flights, he said, were
"the only way we can get this kind of information"—information
he had defined as vital to our security. The flights, he suggested,
would force action at the summit on the Eisenhower "open skies"
plan. "An indication has been made," he said, "that such activities
may have to continue in the future." Yet, while the Vice President
was manfully defending the continuation of the flights, the President himself actually called them off (it was revealed in Paris on
May 16) three days earlier! Why had no one told Nixon? Can it
be that no one thinks of him when it comes time to make big decisions? If this is so, what about "experience"?

The other element of Nixon's supposed foreign policy experience
lies in his foreign tours. It is true that Nixon has covered a lot of
territory. For that matter, Kennedy has visited forty-two countries.
Neither has been charged with diplomatic missions. Kennedy's
trips have probably allowed more time for serious work than
Nixon's, with his all-day schedules of parades, public speeches,
receptions, and banquets. And Nixon's tours can hardly be termed
unparalleled successes, even in terms of crowd reaction. His Latin
American trip was a disaster. This was not just because Nixon was
a *Yanqui*. Adlai Stevenson is a *Yanqui* too, and his South American trip was a triumph. It was because Nixon came to Latin America as a champion of the niggardly and prodictatorship policies of
the Eisenhower administration, and because Nixon failed to convey
emotions of his own appealing enough to overcome that handicap.
Stevenson came as the heir of F.D.R.'s Good Neighbor policy and
through his evident personal commitment showed that Good
Neighborism was not dead in North America.

How about the Nixon trip to the Soviet Union? Nixon, it is

said (and, of course, Lodge too in the United Nations) had unique experience in "standing up" to the Russians. Nixon debated Khrushchev in a kitchen. Lodge debated Gromyko in the Security Council. This, it is supposed, qualifies them uniquely for dealing with the Communists in the decade ahead. But is debating the essence of our problem with the Communist world? "Those who regard the problem of standing up to the Russians as standing up to them in a debate," Walter Lippmann has well said, "do not understand the problem of standing up to the Russians." Assume that Nixon won his debate at the American Exposition in Moscow, he went on: "What were the results of winning this argument and all the other arguments we have won? Has the frontier of freedom advanced one inch? Has the empire of tyranny receded at all? In the year that has passed since Nixon stood up to Khrushchev in Moscow and since Lodge won his debate in New York our position in the Far East has deteriorated seriously and our position in Cuba and in Latin America has certainly not improved."

What does all this prove? It proves that the job of dealing with Communism is not the job of arguing with the Russians. Lippmann states the real issue with precision:

The Russians are for all practical purposes impervious to argument, especially to public argument. Their calculations, which are often far from accurate, are not in terms of words or principles or ideals. Their calculations are made in terms of power—in terms of missiles and tanks, and technical schools and trained engineers, and steel and oil and houses and Sputniks.

Nixon won his debate. Lodge has, so he tells us, won all of his debates. But nevertheless the Communist influence is expanding. Why? Because the struggle between us is not a debate at all. It is a conflict of power against power, and this country has allocated too small a part of too small a product to those public actions which make for national power.

Experience is helpful, especially experience in doing good things. But experience in doing stupid things is no advantage. Experience unilluminated by a grasp of central issues is worse than useless. The question is: which candidate understands what the fundamental problem is of restoring American power and influence in the world? Which has the personal will and the political authority required to persuade the American people to accept the measures essential for our survival as a great and free nation?

Nixon remains a characteristic figure of the Eisenhower period —concerned with externals rather than with substance, indifferent to the merits of issues, generally satisfied with things as they are. There is no reason to suppose that a Nixon administration would be much diff;rent from an Eisenhower administration, except that the public relations would be more efficiently and energetically organized. Kennedy, on the other hand, stands for a new epoch in American politics. He understands that we can't go on as we have in the last decade. He understands that our nation must awaken from the Eisenhower trance and get on the march again. He understands that this requires purpose and sacrifice.

8

THE DISTANCE THE Democratic Party has traveled in a decade may be seen by comparing the favorite slogans of the last Truman years—"you never had it so good" and "don't let them take it away"—with Kennedy's definition of the New Frontier at Los Angeles: "It sums up not what I intend to *offer* the American people, but what I intend to *ask* of them." The Democratic Party underwent a transformation in its years in the wilderness. To a considerable degree that transformation was the work of a single man—Adlai Stevenson. In his eight years as titular leader, Stevenson renewed the Democratic Party. His conviction that affluence was not enough for the good life, his contempt for complacency, his impatience with clichés of the past, his demand for new ideas, his respect for the people who have them, his sense of the complexity of history and the desperate need for leadership set the tone for a new era in Democratic politics.

This was evident in Los Angeles. All the candidates talked more or less in the Stevenson idiom. They all stressed perils, uncertainties, sacrifices, purpose. Though his supporters failed to get him the nomination, historians may well regard Stevenson as the true victor in the convention. He had remade the Democratic Party, and largely in his own image, even if he was not himself to be the beneficiary. More perhaps than either of them fully realizes, Kennedy today is the heir and executor of the Stevenson revolution. It is not only that many of his intellectual advisers are men whom Thomas K. Finletter gathered for Stevenson in the mid-fifties. It is that Kennedy shares the Stevenson vision of a new departure in American life—a time of national revival—that he knows (or believes he knows) what is required to bring it about, and that his passion in life is to preside over its initiation.

This is perhaps the crucial difference between Nixon and Kennedy. Nixon wants to be President, not because he has things in mind which only the President can accomplish, but because, having reached the rung below the top, he is irresistibly impelled to climb to the top of the ladder. He wants to become President because the Presidency is agreeable for its own sake. Once there, he supposes he can figure out what he should do, or not do. The commodity Kennedy seeks to sell is his program; the commodity Nixon seeks to sell is himself.

For Nixon, the Presidency seems essentially a source of private gratification. For Kennedy, it is a means of public achievement. Both men are deeply ambitious. But Kennedy is ambitious because the Presidency alone would give him the power to fulfill purposes which have long lain in his mind and heart.

II   THEIR POLICIES

WHAT ARE THESE purposes? I have indicated some of them along the way. But it might be useful to put the choice of 1960 in sharper outline by comparing the acceptance addresses of the two candidates.

The Nixon address had, of course, the standard subjective touches: the references to "Pat . . . our daughters . . . my mother"; the Hollywood line, "I believe in the American dream because I have seen it come true in my own life." It had the usual politician's gambit, "We are not going to try to outpromise our opponents in this campaign," which, as any student of politics knows, is inexorably followed by a list of splendid promises to young people, old people, wage earners, minorities, and farmers. It had the inevitable bouquets for the Eisenhower administration. Obviously Nixon had to say something nice about Eisenhower; but to credit him with "the best eight-year record of any Administration in the history of this country" may be a trifle excessive— not because he had only been in office seven years and five months, but more particularly because with this statement Nixon was pronouncing Eisenhower a better President than George Washington, Thomas Jefferson, Andrew Jackson, Theodore Roosevelt, Woodrow Wilson, or Franklin Roosevelt. This is an astonishing judgment, even from a loyal member of the team. It is one that Nixon cannot really believe.

What is central for our purposes, however, is (*a*) Nixon's estimate of the present American position and (*b*) what, if anything, he thinks must be done to improve that position. "America," he said, "is the strongest nation militarily, economically, and ideologically in the world today." He noted that there were those who questioned our national superiority; with almost a relapse to the good old rocking-socking days, the Vice President implied that those who did so were Communists. "I say that, at a time the

35

Communists are running us down abroad, it is time to speak up for America at home." If the American position is so idyllic, then obviously nothing very drastic has to be done. Nixon did offer two proposals, in addition to his check list of benefits for special groups. "First, we must take the necessary steps which will assure that the American economy grows at a maximum rate." This is an admirable idea; it should hardly surprise anyone who has read this far that only a month before, at St. Louis, the Vice President sarcastically dismissed the advocates of this very view as men playing "the most fashionable political parlor game of our time—a game we might well call 'growthmanship.' " Nixon's second concrete recommendation was for the unification of all agencies in the foreign field "into one powerful economic and ideological striking force"—a proposal that, so far as anyone has analyzed it, is pure public relations. This exhausted the Nixon agenda. He concluded with passages of agreeable rhetoric about devotion to the great ideals of the American Revolution.

The Kennedy acceptance address was more objective in tone: no references, for example, to wife and family. An unwise excursion into history made Richard Cromwell the nephew of Oliver; he was the son. So far as the central question is concerned, the Kennedy speech took a less roseate view of America's present position. His estimate is the same as Nelson Rockefeller's—"our position in the world today is dramatically weaker than fifteen years ago." Abroad, the balance of power is shifting. "Friends have slipped into neutrality, and neutrals into hostility." There is ferment in the underdeveloped world. At home, Kennedy discerned "a technological revolution on the farm . . . an urban-population revolution . . . a peaceful revolution for human rights . . . a medical revolution [extending] the lives of our elder citizens . . . a revolution of automation." He also discerned "a slippage in our intellectual and moral strength." "Seven lean years of drought and famine have withered the field of ideas." He objected to "the 'payola' mentality, the expense-account way of life, the confusion between what is legal and what is right. Too many Americans have lost their way, their will, and their sense of historic purpose."

Whereas in Nixon's view the times demand only a continuation and mild enlargement of the measures of the Eisenhower administration, Kennedy asserted that we stand "at a turning point in history." "The old era is ending," he said. "The old ways will not do." The Republican pledge "is a pledge to the *status quo*—and today there can be no *status quo*." The times, he said, "demand invention, innovation, imagination, decision."

That is the choice our nation must make, a choice that lies not merely between two men or two parties, but between the public interest and private comfort, between national greatness and national decline, between the fresh air of progress and the stale, dank atmosphere of "normalcy," between determined dedication and creeping mediocrity.

2

FROM THIS AND other Nixon speeches, one can identify the main elements which would constitute the economic policy of a Nixon administration. "We are economic conservatives," Nixon has said; and by this he means primarily that economic power should be wielded by business rather than by government. His mind is well stocked with the economic wisdom of country-club locker-rooms. Take, for example, his pronouncements as chairman since 1959 of the Cabinet Committee on Price Stability for Economic Growth. The Vice President sought this appointment; when he received it, *The New York Times* noted that this was "the closest he has come to formal executive power." According to the *Times* again, Nixon wrote the major report himself. This was the document which *The Washington Post* described as "one of the most redundant, uninspired and generally useless documents lately to come off the government's mimeographing machines." Nixon blamed inflation in conventional businessmen's terms on labor unions, government spending, and farm price supports. He offered three remedies: a congressional resolution opposing inflation and making price stability a goal of government; economy in government spending; and the raising of the ceiling on interest rates. The idea of a resolution is a pure public relations gimmick; it would have given no new powers to anyone to deal with inflation. The

demand for economy ignored the mounting needs for public services and for defense. Raising interest rates would mean only a
continuation of the futile and discriminatory attempt to combat
inflation by tight money. The report made no contribution at all to
the discussion of inflation. No one paid any attention to it. It sank
instantly from sight, like a rock dropped into the Potomac River.
Subsequent minor reports emanating from the committee have
added nothing.

The Vice President sees no defects in the current organization
of the American economy or in the way we currently use our
national wealth.* The injection of "the humble bit" into the
"image" should deceive no one into thinking that, because Nixon
came from economically modest circumstances, he must therefore
have particular sympathy for those he left behind. Quite often the
reverse is true: people who have come from nowhere tend not to
understand why the others who are still back there could not have
risen too; while sons of the rich, wondering why the accident of
birth should make them so much more fortunate than the rest,
sometimes grow deeply concerned with the sufferings of the poor
and the inequities of society. Alexander Hamilton and Herbert
Hoover came from poverty; Thomas Jefferson and Franklin Roosevelt from affluence. Nixon, having seen the American dream "come
true in my own life," may well be inclined to confuse dream with
reality for all.

Thus the Vice President has no use for the notion that too little
of our economic abundance is devoted to public purposes—that is,
to the general welfare. He resists most efforts to invest more in the
public sector. His casting vote killed federal aid for teachers' sal-
aries in 1960. He was a consistent opponent of public housing
throughout his congressional career. He strongly condemned the

---

* Or at least this is the general tenor of his remarks and of his legislative
record. On the other hand, he is also capable of taking the other side of
the argument. Thus, at St. Louis on June 21, 1960: "If we are to grow at a
maximum rate, we must recognize the continuing need for investment in
the public sector." Most of the time, though, he takes the line he took in
Chicago on January 27: "We Republicans have unshakable faith that the
way to achieve these goals is by the free choice of millions of individual
consumers."

Forand Bill to provide medical aid to old people through the Social Security system.

One way of allocating resources, of course, is the tax system; and Nixon's tax proposals show succinctly in what direction and to whom he thinks our national wealth should be steered. Thus he calls for "lower rates in the higher income brackets." He would replace excise taxes with a general manufacturers' sales tax. He also favors larger depreciation allowances and faster tax write-offs for businessmen. Such measures would obviously help wealthy individuals. They also, Nixon contends, would produce a higher rate of economic growth.

One of the problems of growth rates is that "gross national product" is a statistical measure which weighs a million dollars' worth of cosmetics equally with a million dollars' worth of hospitals or missiles. The Nixon proposals might well increase the gross national product by stimulating the production of more lipstick and eye shadow. But our present shortage in the United States is not a shortage of consumer goods. It is a shortage of things which the private economy does not and, in the main, cannot provide—everything from schools to atomic submarines. The problem obviously is to steer our fantastic wealth into areas where, instead of serving national self-indulgence, it builds national power. This is the problem which Nixon has resolutely ignored. Nothing he has ever publicly said even acknowledges its existence.

As Kennedy's invocation of a choice between "the public interest and private comfort" suggests, it is a problem to which he has devoted much thought. By assigning too little of our economic output to national purposes, he feels, we have starved the sinews of national strength. The answer, he believes, lies in an active determination to achieve a high level of balanced national growth, not a lopsided growth in which consumer luxuries shoot ahead while public needs go unmet. He would intend to keep standards of living rising steadily, especially for the poorer families in the country; but he would devote a large share of the increments of growth to repairing the deficit in our public services. He has no preference for a government per se; indeed, he would probably take steps to deflate such swollen and monstrous bureaucratic growths as the

Pentagon; but he rightly doubts whether private enterprise is going to supply all the things we need to assure our national strength.

Above all, he realizes that national strength includes much more than armies and weapon systems. It depends essentially on long-run factors—on the education and health of our people, on the guarantee of their equal opportunity, on the growth of our economy, on the development of our resources. These all seem to him wise and necessary objects of national investment. Nor does he feel that such things can be postponed to some more propitious time. The longer we wait, the harder it will be to solve our problems. As Lippmann has said, "Once you've failed to educate a child, you've failed, and you can't make that up later." Kennedy's view, it is clear, is that affirmative Presidential leadership is desperately required—to bring about, through the traditional democratic means of Congressional action, a better allocation of our resources; to assure equal rights to all our citizens; to revolutionize the moral tone of the country; to inaugurate the new epoch of national progress.

3

THE NATIONAL REVIVAL, as Kennedy sees it, is not just a matter of domestic interest. It is of the most vital concern in our foreign affairs, since only a moral and intellectual revival within the United States can charge our foreign policy with the spirit of creative idealism necessary to restore the confidence of other peoples in our purposes.

Kennedy is surely right. It is no accident that America has had its most effective moments of world leadership when our foreign policy has expressed a visible reality of American performance. The words of Wilson and Roosevelt went straight to the minds and hearts of the people of the world, while the words of Eisenhower and Nixon fall on deaf ears, not because Wilson and Roosevelt had better words (though this was the case too), but because their words were underwritten by their deeds. The fact that Wilson and Roosevelt had fought hard for freedom and opportunity and social justice in their own land earned them the right to talk about such matters to the world. It was Wilson's New Freedom which validated his Fourteen Points, as it was Roosevelt's New Deal which validated his Four Freedoms. The effect of TVA, for example, on the imagination of aspiring peoples everywhere has been incalculable. It is Adlai Stevenson's record as an American liberal which makes his the most influential American voice to the outside world today. But what is authentic idealism on the lips of men who have won the right to talk about freedom and opportunity and social justice becomes the sheerest moralism and hypocrisy when uttered to the world by people notably indifferent to such things in their own land. Men who address righteous sermons to the world while at home they tolerate McCarthy and Little Rock and West Virginia poverty and the rest are bound to strike others as ineffectual figureheads or sanctimonious frauds.

It is one of Kennedy's strengths that he sees foreign policy as an extension of a nation's domestic existence. He knows that one cannot be forward-looking in the world and backward-looking (or even stationary) in the United States. If our foreign policy in recent years has been defensive and unconvincing, it is because we have temporarily been a conservative nation, dedicated to holding what we have, devoid of larger ideas or purposes. Nelson Rockefeller has well characterized the Eisenhower-Dulles-Nixon foreign policy:

We have been tempted to act largely in terms of reaction rather than creation. We have seemed too often to lack coherent and continuing purpose. Rather, we have relied on sporadic responses to sudden needs and crises. . . .

We have tended to imagine that broad general declarations of national intention would affect the world by their mere pronouncement. Perhaps we have been dreaming that words could be substituted for deeds, problems be patched up with slogans, abstract proclamations take the place of concrete and creative policies.

This policy is lavish with words and languid with deeds. We are forever "behind" events, seeking grimly to catch up, instead of ahead of them, in a position of leadership and initiative. To be "tough" with the Russians means a display of indignation, not a display of strength. The Republicans are twentieth century mandarins, shooting at the barbarians with paper guns and spending the national substance building summer palaces.

An age of "invention, innovation, imagination, decision" might change all this. A new spirit rising within our nation will lead to a reconstruction of our approach to foreign affairs. Instead of responding interminably to the initiatives of others, we will begin to take the initiative ourselves in the fight for a decent peace. Disarmament, instead of being an occupation for clerks, will receive the top priority it deserves in the conduct of our foreign affairs. Pending the establishment of a reliable disarmament system, of course, we have no choice but to remove the existing gaps in our own defenses; indeed, only by showing that we can stay in the arms race as long as they, can we convince the Russians of the imperative need for arms control. But we will arm in order to disarm. Our emphasis in foreign aid will shift from providing undeveloped countries with guns to providing them the economic and technical assistance essential for their own economic growth. Within the hemisphere, we will stop honoring dictators and start supporting democracies.

The key to peace does not lie in just talking, in the Nixon manner, about "the great ideals of the American Revolution." The key to peace lies in *doing* something about those ideals—in showing the world that the American Revolution is not dead in the land of its birth. It lies in leadership that will put American idealism to work. Let no one be deceived about this: many of the things such leadership will have to do will grievously offend the "economic conservatives" of America. Nothing in Nixon's record or utterance suggests that he has the desire or the stamina to risk such offense. Kennedy, on the other hand, well understands the bitter necessity of decision. So do the remarkable group of foreign policy leaders in the Democratic Party—Adlai Stevenson, Chester Bowles, Thomas Finletter, Averell Harriman, Hubert Humphrey, Mike Mansfield, J. William Fulbright, Dean Acheson. That is why the best hope for a secure, just, and stable peace rests in the election of Kennedy and a Democratic administration.

III   THEIR PARTIES

In our quadrennial elections, the American nation chooses not only individuals, but parties. Parties acquire identities, like people; and history has endowed each of our national parties with a distinctive personality and philosophy. This character derives in great part from the relationship of the party with the interests which it represents; for, as Madison pointed out in *The Federalist:* "a landed interest, a manufacturing interest, a mercantile interest, a moneyed interest, with many lesser interests, grow up of necessity in civilized nations," and "the regulation of these various and interfering interests forms the principal task of modern legislation, and involves the spirit of party and faction in the necessary and ordinary operations of the government."

Thus from the beginning, when the Virginia planters made their alliance with the workingmen of New York, the Democratic Party has typically been a coalition of diverse interests, united by opposition to control of the government by the most powerful group in the community. Everything else about the Democratic Party follows from its multi-interest character. What was an implicit conception of the party with Jefferson became more explicit with Jackson. In later years Bryan and Wilson revitalized the theory of the Democratic Party as an alliance of the lesser groups against rule by the dominant economic group; and under Franklin D. Roosevelt, of course, this pluralistic conception reached its fulfillment.

What is the essence of a multi-interest administration? It is surely that the leading interests in society are all represented in the interior processes of policy formation—which can be done only if members or advocates of these interests are included in key positions of government. The Roosevelt and Truman administrations functioned as working expressions of American pluralism. The farmers, the laboring men, the intellectuals, and the nonconformist businessmen were all represented in the government; and the poli-

43

ticians played their proper roles as the harmonizers of divergent interests. It is sometimes forgotten that Roosevelt appointed three Republicans to his Cabinet in 1933; and at no time in the thirties and forties was the business community without powerful representatives within the Democratic administrations. The presence of the Jesse Joneses, T. Jefferson Coolidges, John W. Haneses, Forrestals, Knudsens, Claytons, and the rest was often a source of anguish to die-hard New Dealers. But they were there nonetheless. Roosevelt had an instinctive recognition that, however much he might detest the official leadership of the business community, he needed the cooperation and support of businessmen of good will.

A multi-interest party has several obvious advantages from the viewpoint of providing wise national leadership. The first is that, since policy emerges from a wide consultation among various groups, it has a much better chance of corresponding to the needs of a diversified society and a sprawling nation. If government programs have to run the gantlet of a variety of interests, the resulting process of criticism and modification increases the chance of producing policies that will genuinely serve the national interest. Of course, a single interest may be gifted with infallibility and thus not require the correction of other viewpoints; but this situation has not yet arisen in the American democracy, where, as Jefferson has reminded us, we have not found angels to govern us.

The second advantage of the multi-interest party springs from the premium the coalition situation places on strong leadership. The driver with a team of fractious and competing horses must learn to impose his will if he is to stay on the road. Similarly a party leader who first must master his own coalition is more likely to develop the authority that would enable him to lead the country. The potential viciousness of the multi-interest system lies in the possibility that a political leader might cater only to the interest groups and let the national welfare vanish in a scramble for special benefits. The "pressure-group state" is a real threat, and not to be underestimated. But the experience of subduing these varied appetites only further develops capacities for strong leadership. Nothing produces a more lively sense of the public interest than an awareness of the conflicts among special interests. The experience of directing a multi-interest party, in short, is unparalleled training for the experience of governing a multi-interest nation.

The third advantage of the multi-interest party springs from the premium the coalition situation places on ideas—that is, on thought and on *thinking*. This is partly because the intellectuals, as a permanent minority group, will always be members of the multi-interest coalition. It is also because of the inherent need of the multi-interest party for policies, programs, formulas which will bind divergent groups together and reconcile their conflicting interests. Above all, the lesser interests of society are ordinarily less welded to the *status quo*. They feel a need for change and in so feeling keep public leadership in tune with the importunities of history. "He that will not apply new remedies must expect new evils," wrote Bacon: "for time is the greatest innovator." The multi-interest party, in short, has both an urgent need for ideas and the people on hand who can work them out; and the result will be a much higher degree of intellectual activity and creativity.

The fourth advantage of the multi-interest party is that it has a better chance of winning consent for its policies. This is partly because these policies, developed from a concurrence of groups, are more likely to meet the needs of all; and partly because the multi-interest process of policy formation has an inherent tendency to secure assent since no group in the country is likely to have the feeling of total exclusion.

For better or worse, popular consent, intellectual vitality, and strong Presidential leadership are characteristics of multi-interest administrations. And the fact that the Democratic Party is basically a coalition of interests gives that party its special flavor—its inner contentiousness, its rowdiness, its compassion, its closeness to popular concern and popular feeling.

2

THUS THE DEMOCRATIC PARTY through our history (save for the decades of the 1850's and 1860's) has been the custodian of the miscellany of lesser interests in our nation. So too, from the beginning, when Alexander Hamilton declared his faith in the "rich and well-born" and worked to link "the interest of the State in an intimate connection with those of the rich individuals belonging to it," the conservative party, whether called Federalist, Whig, or Republican, has been typically a party based on a single interest. The Republican Party, in particular, except for the few years when it embraced the cause of antislavery, has characteristically identified the general welfare with the welfare of the most powerful group in our society—the business community. It has been, as Emerson said of the Whigs, "the shop-and-till party." When business took over the British Conservative Party in 1903 and Winston Churchill crossed the aisle to join the Liberals, he predicted the transformation of Conservatism into a new party, "like perhaps the Republican Party in the United States . . . rigid, materialist and secular, whose opinion will turn on tariffs and who will cause the lobbies to be crowded with the touts of protected industries."

Just as its coalition base of Southern farmers and Northern city workers determines the character of the Democratic Party, so its single-interest base determines the character of the Republican Party. Representing the organized wealth of the country, it has a vast stake in keeping things unchanged; this has made it the party of the *status quo*. Representing the most powerful private interest, it has more influence than any other group and thus less need for the protection of the state; this has made it the party of negative government. Representing the *status quo* and negative government, it reveres clichés and distrusts ideas; this has made it, like the old British Tory Party, the "stupid party." Excluding labor leaders, farmers, and intellectuals from its policy-making councils, it is under an irresistible compulsion to mistake a class interest for the national interest, to suppose that what is good for General Motors is good for the country; this has distorted its views of the national welfare. Lacking the chastening experience of mingling with other segments of the population, it takes its own pretensions with the utmost solemnity; this has made it the party of stiff collars, stuffed shirts, and fogies, old and young. ("To the Republicans," Anne O'Hare McCormick once wrote, "politics is a business, while to the Democrats it's a pleasure.")

The genius of the Republican Party, in short, has consisted in being the political embodiment of organized conservatism—opposed to change, to affirmative and creative statecraft, to new ideas, to interpretations of the general welfare that might conflict with vested profits or cherished platitudes. The basic trouble is *not* that the Republican Party represents the business community, however. The trouble is that it represents a *single* interest. I would object just as strongly to a party which addressed itself exclusively to the welfare of labor or of farmers (or, for that matter, of college professors). No form of single-interest government can do justice to the inexhaustible variety of a multi-interest country. It is because thoughtful businessmen understand this that so many of them have become valued and influential members of the Democratic coalition.

Nor do I suggest that the Republican Party has been a single-interest party at every moment in its existence. It was not so under Lincoln or under Theodore Roosevelt. Twenty years ago Wendell Willkie made a gallant try at reconstructing the Grand Old Party. But the modern efforts to broaden the base of the Republican Party have all ended in failure. As T.R. put it when he walked out of the G.O.P. in 1912:

There is absolutely nothing to be said for government by a plutocracy, for government by men very powerful in certain lines and gifted with the money touch, but with ideals which in their essences are merely those of so many glorified pawnbrokers.

For seven and a half years, the Eisenhower administration has given us a copybook demonstration of the meaning of single-interest government—from the moment when President Eisenhower's first Secretary of the Interior proclaimed: "We're here in the saddle as an administration representing business and industry."

The belief that successful businessmen have cornered the wisdom necessary for running an infinitely diversified country is reflected, for example, in the President's choice of his Cabinet, his advisers, even of the guests at his stag dinners. For all the "President-of-all-the-people" flourishes in Eisenhower's speeches, he has appointed many fewer non-Republicans and nonbusinessmen to high office than Franklin Roosevelt appointed Republicans and businessmen at the highest tide of the New Deal. No President since Hoover has restricted his contacts to so narrow a circle; Mr. Eisenhower has even held his relations with the professional politicians of his own party to a minimum. One shudders to think what would have happened if a Democratic President had chosen all his advisers and cronies from the trade union movement or from the universities. Yet the values of a business culture remain so dominant that few seem to mind the fact that for over seven years the President of the United States has received his information and his advice from so unvaried a body of Americans.

But this would be all right, if the information and advice were good. The danger of so guileless a faith in the infallibility of successful businessmen is reflected most disastrously in the resulting conception of our national priorities. President Eisenhower's guiding purpose—repeatedly endorsed by Vice President Nixon—has been to maximize private spending. As Dr. Raymond J. Saulnier, chairman of the President's Council of Economic Advisers, set forth his theory of the American economy to the Joint Economic Committee, "Its ultimate purpose is to produce more consumer goods. This is the goal. This is the object of everything that we are working at: to produce things for consumers." Everything, except the most urgent needs of national defense, has been sacrificed to this.

In 1954 the President stated his goal: "We will reduce the share of the national income which is spent by the government." The first result was the Revenue Act of 1954, which transferred some $7 billion ($10 billion in current dollars) from public to private spending—that is, from schools and missiles to gadgets and gimmicks. He has repeatedly stated his conviction that private spending is always better than public spending:

Our Federal money will never be spent so intelligently and in so useful a fashion for the economy as will the expenditures that would be made by the private taxpayer, if he hadn't had so much of it funneled off into the Federal Government.

All this follows from the Presidential delusion that a single interest has a monopoly of social wisdom. His business friends tell him that private spending is productive and virtuous, while public spending is inflationary and wicked; that the economy can "afford" to tear down fancy office buildings in order to put up fancier ones, but that it can't "afford" to clear noisome slums and put up decent public housing; that we can "afford" as a people to spend $10 billion a year on advertising but can't "afford" to spend more than $3.5 billion a year on higher education; that government retrenchment—that is, freeing as much money as possible for private spending so things can be sold at a profit to consumers—is more important than providing for our military security or for meeting the social needs of a swiftly growing population.

And all this is part of a larger delusion—that government is somehow the enemy, and that it is better to watch slums multiply, segregation persist, education decay, West Virginia miners starve, pollution spread, and the Soviet Union occupy the moon than to give the government the resources to prevent these scandals or bring them to an end.

Single-interest government has starved the public needs of the nation, from our military security to our provisions for the welfare and opportunity of future generations. It has created the paradox of public squalor in the midst of private opulence. It has produced a prevailing materialism which has debased our tradition and corrupted our morals.

It has crippled our position in the world, not just by denying resources to defense and foreign aid, but above all by presenting America to the world in the image of self-righteous, complacent, and sterile conservatism rather than of the clearheaded and tough-minded idealism that brought the Republic into being.

Government poised on so narrow a basis can never generate the sense of glowing national purpose essential to the expansion of justice and opportunity at home and to the recovery of leadership abroad. The time has come for America to have a government that will express the wonderfully various character and interests of our people and will thereby release the creative and magnanimous energies of our nation.

3

THE NATURE OF the party affects the performance of the candidate. It affects the character of his advice and the character of his obligations. Nixon would come to the White House surrounded by the same kind of men who have surrounded Eisenhower—a few more politicians among them, perhaps, but politicians deeply imbued with the ethos of single-interest government. Would his banker friends often demand that President Nixon lower the interest rate and thus reduce their profits? Would the owners of television stations insist that the Federal Communications Commission be run in the public interest? Would the Wall Street brokers complain about the laxity of the Securities and Exchange Commission? Would his guests from General Motors and du Pont call for more energetic enforcement of the antitrust laws? Would the potentates of the American Medical Association urge adequate federal plans to improve medical care? Would men sworn to faith in the balanced budget want a larger degree of public investment? Would men whose every instinct recoils at the thought of affirmative government desire strong Presidential leadership and strong national policies? To do what must be done, Nixon would have to run counter to every force in his immediate environment. His whole career of "other-direction"—not to speak of his own commitment to economic conservatism—suggests how unlikely such a defiance would be.

As the Republican Party is the party of the Establishment, so Nixon is the candidate of the Establishment. The Establishment, because it is happily established, seeks no important change in anything. If everything is fine just as it is in the United States, then Nixon is the man for President.

Kennedy, on the other hand, stands for change, not only because of personal conviction, but because of the forces whom he represents, with whom he would consult and to whom he would be indebted. As I have said, I make no claim that minor interests enjoy any superior virtue over the major interest. Individual labor leaders, for example, have shown qualities of greed as reprehensible as those of any robber baron. Yet Kennedy's long fight in the Senate for labor reform has clearly demonstrated an independence of the trade unions; and one advantage of a multi-interest coalition over a single-interest party is that its leader need not become the prisoner of any single group. The influences which would play on Kennedy would inevitably reinforce his own inclination to advance the public interest and to plan, not for the short-run welfare of one group, but for the long-run welfare of the entire nation.

4

KENNEDY AND NIXON stand in sharp contrast—in their personalities, their progress, and their parties. Each asks the American people to repose in him the command of our national policy over the next four years. With Nixon, personality, programs, and party combine to create the expectation of a static government dominated by the forces in our society most opposed to change. With Kennedy, personality, policies, and party combine to create the expectation of an affirmative government dominated by intelligence and vision and dedicated to abolishing the terrifying discrepancy between the American performance and the American possibility. No political leader can guarantee anything, and no one can guarantee any political leader. But the election of Kennedy, like that of Wilson in 1912 and Franklin Roosevelt in 1933, would plainly keep open vital options in our life. Upon our capacity to *move* in the next four years lies our chance of meeting the challenge of Communism, of providing a decency of life and opportunity for our own sons and daughters, and of maintaining our nation as the last, best hope of freedom.

The choice we confront in 1960 is to muddle along as we have done for a decade, watching our power and influence decline in the world and our own country sink into mediocrity and cant and payola and boredom—either this or to recover control over our national destiny and resume the movement to fulfill the real promise of American life, a promise defined not by the glitter of our wealth but by the splendor of our ideals.

Printed in the United States
By Bookmasters